SCHIRMER'S LIBRARY
OF MUSICAL CLASSICS

FRANZ WOHLFAHRT

Op. 45

Sixty Studies

For the Violin

Edited by

GASTON BLAY

IN TWO BOOKS

G. SCHIRMER, Inc.

DISTRIBUTED BY

HAL•LEONARD®
CORPORATION
7777 W. BLUEMOUND RD. P.O. BOX 13819 MILWAUKEE, WI 53213

Etuden. | Studies.

Revised by
Theodore John

⊓ Herunterstrich. | ⊓ Down - bow.
∨ Hinaufstrich. | ∨ Up - bow.

Franz Wohlfahrt. Cp. 45, Book II.

Nº 31. Moderato.

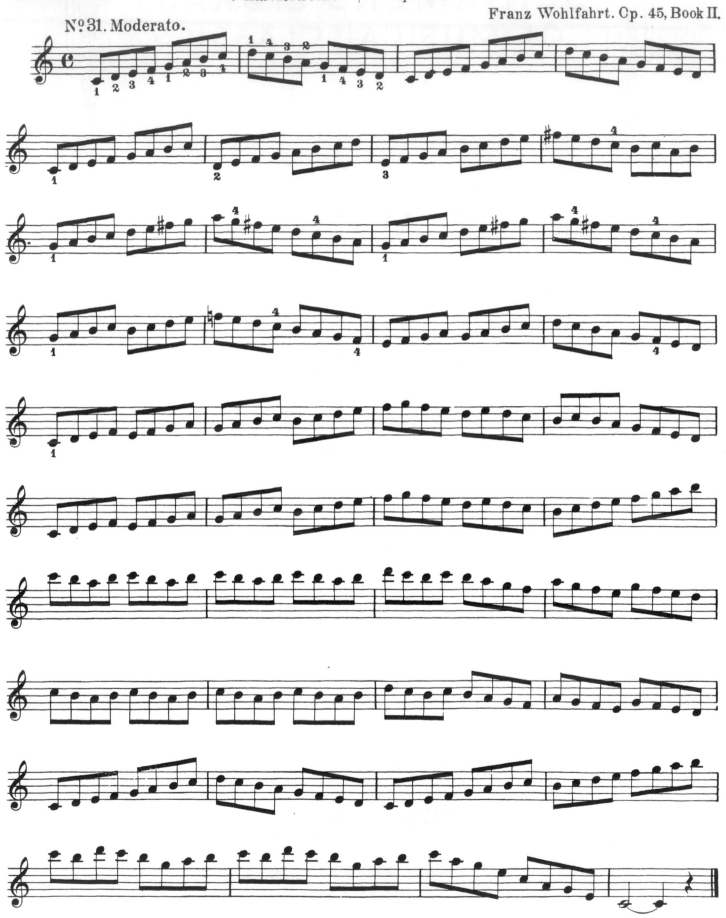

№ 33. Allegro moderato.

№ 34. Allegro.

№ 35. Allegro.

No. 36. Moderato.

No. 37. Moderato.

№ 38. Moderato.

Nº 39. Moderato.

Nº 40. **Allegro scherzando.** Springender Bogen.
Springing bow (ricochet)

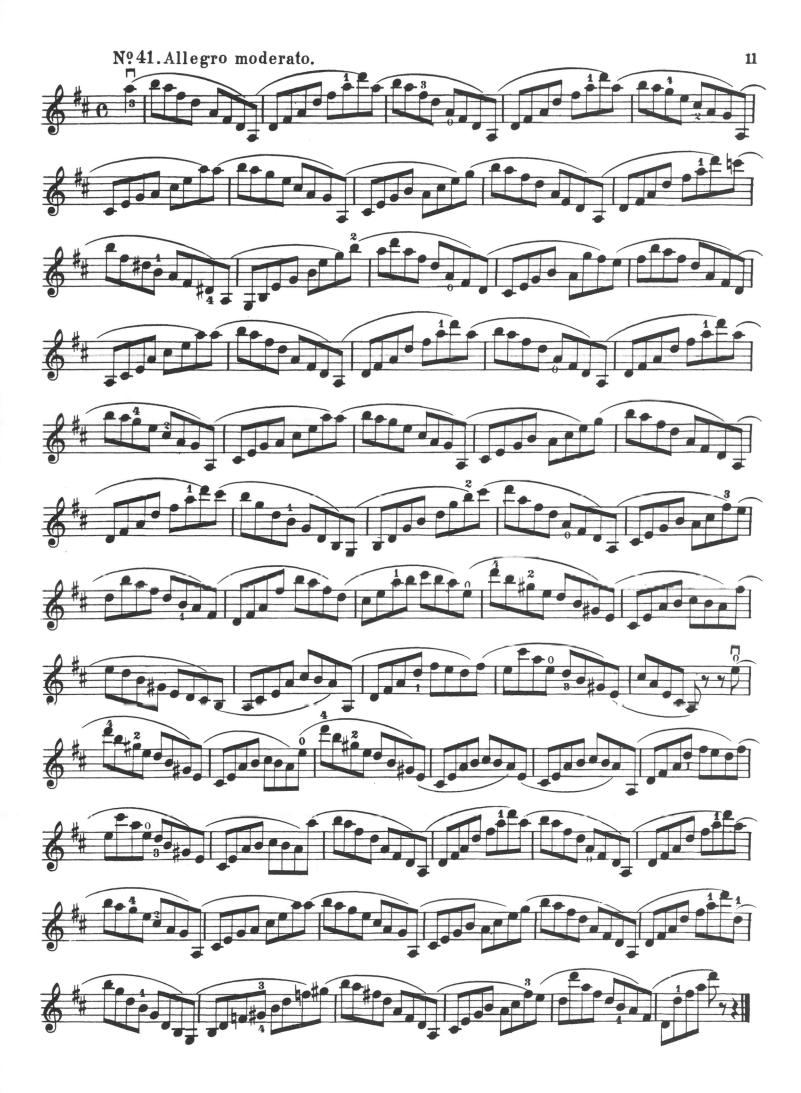

Nº 41. Allegro moderato.

№ 42. Andante.

№ 43. Moderato.

14

Nº 44. Tempo di marcia.

Nº45. Moderato.

№46. Allegro.

Nº 47. Andante cantabile.

18 № 48. Allegretto.

№ 49. Allegro.

№ 50. Allegro.

№51. Moderato.

Nº 52. Andante.

Nº 53. Andante.

cre - - scen - - do

23

No 54. Allegro.

№ 55. Allegro.

Nº 56. Andante.

№ 57. Moderato assai.

№ 58. Andante.

№ 59. Moderato assai.

№ 60. Allegro con fuoco.

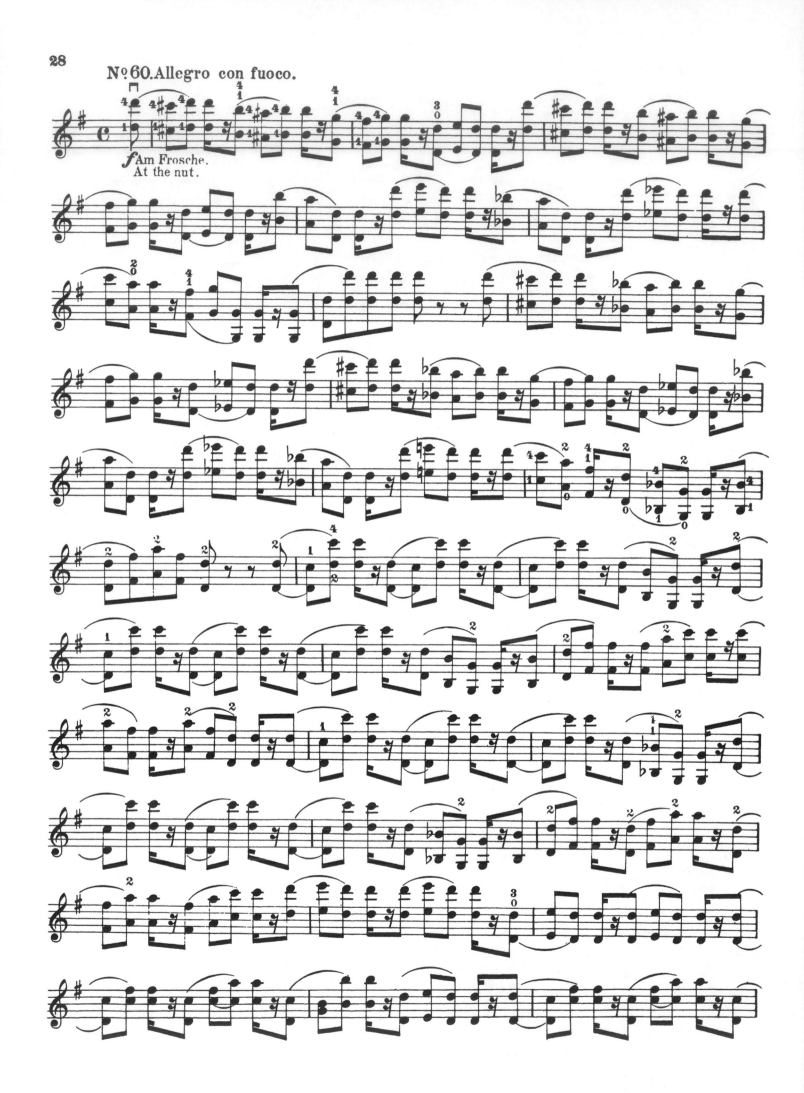

f Am Frosche.
At the nut.